Alexandria's Poetry and Prayers

Alexandria Jett

Alexandria's Poetry And Prayers

Alexandria Jett

Copyright Pending 2024 ©

This publication may not be reproduced, stored in an electronic system, or transmitted in any form or by any means, electronic, mechanical, photocopy, recording, or otherwise, without proper credit to the author. Brief quotations may be used without permission.

Woodsong Publishing, Seymour, IN

Printed in the United States of America

ISBN 978-1-961482-09-8

Table Of Contents

Introduction — VI

Section I—Brokenness — 9
Memories — 9
Anonymously Broken — 10
Withdrawn — 10
Safe Trading — 11
Guiding Me Through The Storm — 11
Torn Into Pieces — 11
My Absence — 12
Missed Opportunities — 12
Grieving Your Loss — 13
Broken Dreams — 13

Section II—Love And Loss — 14
Valentine's Day — 14
Lost and Confused — 14
God Do You See Me? — 15
No Longer Holding Back — 15
Feeling Remorseful — 16
Toxic Love — 16
Living In A Cell — 17
Sealed Lips — 17
Get Off The Merry-Go-Round — 18
Defeat — 18
Loneliness — 19
Deserted Island — 19
Long Lost Love — 20
Rejection — 20
Finding The Wrong People — 21
I Give Myself Away — 21
Too Deep For A Shallow World — 22

I Can No Longer Keep It All Inside	22
Falling For Frineds	23
Hope	23
People Can't Heal You	24
Fallen Stars	24
Grabbing Onto Real Hope	25
Section III—Fear And Anxiety	**26**
Anxious Without You	26
Boogeyman	26
Foot In Mouth	27
Open Book	27
Don't Let Your Mind Deceive You	28
Life Doesn't Stop	28
Sleep Deprivation	29
Bonus Mom	29
Section IV—Loss Of Love	**30**
Love That Didn't Push Through	30
The Storm Is Coming	30
Long Gone	30
Naïve	31
Missing You	32
Dear Romeo	32
Stronger Than The Circumstances	33
Section V—Love	**34**
Self-love	34
Sweet Friend	34
Grace	35
First Love	35
Compromising	36
Our Fate	36
Buried Treasure	37

Real Love	37
The Strength Of Your Love	38
Unbreakable	38
Take A Chance On Love	39
You Have My Heart	39
I Miss All Of You	40
When You Came Back	40
Anniversary Of Knowing You	40
Section VI—Spiritual	**42**
Why Am I Running From You	42
Unfulfilled	42
Who Do You Say That I Am	43
When Will I Find Freedom	43
Satan's A Liar	44
God's Grace	44
Let Go, Let God	45
Freeing Love	45
Forgotten Treasure	46
Similar Struggles	46
Relinquishing Control	47
Don't Get Distracted	47
Listen To What Faith Has To Say	47
You're The Game Changer	48
Complete Surrender	48
Make Over	49
More Of You	49
Stronger On The Other Side	50
A Note From The Author	**51**

Introduction

Hello there. My name is Alexandria Jett. I have a former friend, a spiritual influence in my life, who used to tell me that my poetry was like prayers to God. Her name was Pauline Miller. She's no longer with us, but her legacy and influence still live on to this day. I began writing poetry when I was fourteen years old. I have been writing now for twenty-one years. Writing has been my saving grace. When I couldn't express myself in any other way, I was able to express myself through my poetry. I found my voice through my writing.

I was a backwards, awkward, shy, and troubled child. I grew up with trauma, and I was exposed to the ugliness of the world way too soon in life, much like many others were. At the age of three I witnessed my mother being abused by my father when he got out of prison. I experienced some abuse myself from both of my parents at a young age. I also witnessed what substance abuse was as a child. My father was in and out of jail and prison throughout my childhood for doing numerous types of drugs: from pills to cocaine, and even as extreme as meth. My mom was an alcoholic. She had a very traumatizing childhood herself and never really sought out help or had her own coping mechanism to escape her taunting past. She had been in foster homes, torn apart from her family, and never really knew her identity because her father didn't give his last name to her. To this day, she still feels the pain of rejection from him. She's confused—out of all the children he had—why she couldn't have his last name.

When you don't have an outlet, coping skills, or even God to rely on, it's easy to turn to other things to fill in the void. When my mother was with her biological parents, her father was very abusive. Have you ever heard that expression, "hurt people, hurt people?" That's what happened with

Introduction

my mom. She didn't have stable parents to model what parenthood should look like. She didn't always know how to be nurturing because the little girl in her wasn't nurtured herself. She always tried her best. During her low times, she had a raging war within herself that was too much for her to bear. She was on edge and easily provoked. During those highly stressful times, moments of anxiety, and chaos, she, herself, was an abusive parent—especially when under the influence of alcohol. Fast-forward to when I was fourteen, my mom gave me my first black eye. My sister and I had a friend stay the night, and she told me to take off my glasses. She knew what she was about to do and didn't want to break my glasses. After all, that would cost more money and create more stress. My friend reported this to the school officer, and that was on her permanent record. He said, "You can spank their bottoms, but you cannot hit them in their face." So, sure enough, that made her more upset, and she broke the wooden paddle on my butt.

I tell you this to lead up to why I started writing in the first place. This backstory isn't for your pity but an understanding of why writing was my saving grace. I was a hurting teen, felt rejected by many, and it first started in my own home. I tried cutting my wrists a few times anytime my emotions, anxiety, or feelings became too big to handle on my own. It was only to take the edge off momentarily. I didn't need a short-term solution though; I needed a long-term solution to cope with the heaviness of life. I remember praying to God that if He saw me right where I was and knew all that I was going through, He would send a friend to me to show me He knew right where I was and that I was not alone. He brought Megan Enis into my life at church. She had the gift of knowledge, and God spoke to her about only things He knew about. What I prayed to Him that day, God revealed it to her, and she told me everything I prayed

Introduction

about that Sunday afternoon. She told me that God knew right where I was, and that He loved me and was there for me. After that encounter with her, I began to write. It was like a lightbulb moment, and it all came to me so naturally. I wrote poem after poem, and it was very therapeutic. That was the defining moment in my relationship with God. He showed me that He knew who I was, and where I was in my life, and He helped me through my journey.

As human beings, we all deal with several different emotions in our lives. And if you're a lady, you can experience several different emotions throughout the day. This book will convey poetry for the different emotions I experience daily. Each section or chapter will be of one emotion. For example, one chapter may just be about sadness, while another chapter is about happiness. One section may be about love, while another is about loss. You get the picture. I hope you enjoy my poetry and my prayers.

Alexandria

Brokenness

Memories

Memories flood through my mind,
Of the years I carried all the weight.
The past was so unkind,
With the pressures of life being on my plate.
I was just a child,
Not supposed to know a drunken mother's abuse,
Vivid flashbacks were wild,
Reminding me of how I became a recluse.
My sister and I would find you on the lawn,
Passed out without a clue.
We'd get you in before dawn,
So the neighbours wouldn't see you.
We'd clean you up and make sure you were okay,
Sometimes we were late for our first class,
Sometimes it would happen every day,
And you would give us so much sass.
You were in denial,
Not admitting that anything was wrong.
It was as if you were senile,
Because you forgot you were stuck in a rut for so long.
Years had passed,
Often you'd get in trouble with the law.
DUIs would come fast,
And finally, you had a wake-up call.
It's been a year,
Without a single drop.
All due to prayer,
You made it out on top.
(Sober since 10-5-20)

Alexandria Jett

Anonymously Broken

Piece by piece I'm falling apart,
When will someone heal this shattered heart?
All alone, I'm consumed by fear,
I don't know what I'm capable of when nobody's near.
There's too much turmoil and chaos in my mind,
Why do people in life have to be so unkind?
Nobody said I expected rainbows and a picket fence,
Or a fairytale life that all makes sense.
But when will I feel somewhat whole,
Somewhat complete in my soul.
Why must I always feel so alone,
In this cruel world, I'm on my own.

Withdrawn

This pain is too real,
Everything I keep inside.
I can't bear to feel,
Everything I have to hide.
Constant feelings of rejection,
From everyone I meet.
Where do I go for direction,
If everyone else is elite?
I believed in love,
When it didn't work out before.
Thought it came from above,
Even after every closed door.
But to open myself up again,
Will only lead to more pain.
I can't bear to let anyone else in,
So I'll just have to refrain.

Safe Trading

We've always guarded our hearts,
Keeping everyone at arm's length.
Protecting ourselves when one departs,
Thinking our walls gave us strength.
Shielding us from pain,
There are so many things we keep inside,
But what is there to gain,
When it's our feelings that we hide?

Guiding Me Through the Storm

Life's like a hurricane, sweeping over me,
Spinning faster and faster, uncontrollably.
I try to hold on but it's taking me off course,
The wind's picking up and grabbing me by force.
Vigorously blowing me in every which direction,
I search for landing until I find Your protection.

Torn into Pieces

When you're torn into a million pieces,
From the disappointments of life tearing you apart.
You start to believe your face value decreases,
When others see your shattered heart.
Some may think you're "too broken,"
Something inside of you cannot be fixed.
The damage is done is what's been spoken,
People moved on and you've been nixed.
Searching for someone to be your glue,
To make you whole like before.

You hand over another piece of you,
Only to find another closed door.
You begin to lose hope,
Can't see the sun beyond the clouds.
Going down a slippery slope,
Until you search for the One beyond the crowds.

My Absence

Would you notice if I weren't around,
Or go on about your day?
If I no longer made a sound,
Would you have anything to say?
Some avoid me when I'm here,
Pretend not to see me from afar.
Does anyone even care,
If I cut deeper into each scar?
They always show interest when I do for them,
Take but never give in return.
Cast judgment and condemn,
Not showing the love that I yearn.

Missed Opportunities

Have you ever missed what could've been,
The hope of something real?
The bond that almost began,
The possibility to feel!
But you never hold your breath,
Because eventually, the other shoe will drop,
What could have been has reached it's depth,
Eventually, everything will stop.

Grieving Your Loss

I hate this time of the year,
It leaves a wet pillowcase wishing you were here.
Dreaming of you and hearing your voice,
Why did you have to leave if not by choice?
You left a void in my heart as each day passed by,
The memory of your love will go on, as I look to the sky.
But you're no longer in pain is a simple reminder,
To live each day to the fullest and always be kinder.
(In memory of Jackie Jett, 5/29/18)

Broken Dreams

I lay to rest my dreams of motherhood,
For it's not what you saw in your future, understood.
I say goodbye to the idea of holding you in my arms and squeezing you so tight,
I say goodbye to the idea of tucking you in each night.
To being a caretaker, nurturing a sweet baby,
To have the chance to have endless love but still hold out for that "maybe."
But if I never have that opportunity for those dreams to come true,
Just know I'll never stop loving the idea of you.

Love And Loss

Valentine's Day Loss

This day is about love but all I feel is lost,
I'd do anything not to feel this pain no matter what the cost.
Take these tears of sorrow,
And bring me hope for tomorrow.
Because I don't want to feel this low,
I have to let it go.
Today is just another day so why the pressure of it being something more,
Valentine's Day isn't the only day of love to explore.

Lost and Confused

Why do I associate love with physical touch,
Why do I crave affection so much?
Like that is supposed to heal all that's broken deep down inside,
That eliminates the feelings of wanting to run and hide.
Physical touch isn't what will complete me,
So why am I addicted to the feeling as if it'll set me free?
Each time I give in to that craving for what I had before,
Leaves me empty inside longing for more.
Your touch can never be enough to substitute love,
Your touch can't be what all dreams are made of.

God, Do You See Me?

Could You identify me from a crowd,
Would You even know my face?
If I were to call for You out loud,
Would it be my voice that You would trace?
When I'm sinking in despair,
Needing a guiding hand to reach out.
Could I count on You to be there,
When I'm consumed by worry and doubt?
Could You help me find direction,
When I have lost my way?
In search for Your protection,
To keep the storms of life at bay.
Could You mend a broken heart,
Because this pain is too real?
When everything falls apart,
Will You allow peace to be still?

No Longer Holding Back

I've been holding back for so long,
Trying to find my place where I belong.
Going back and forth to find where I fit,
I second-guess myself, trying to find my grit.
But I've decided to push aside all of my fears,
To take the plunge after all these years.
Finally going after what feels right,
True authenticity with all of my might.
No longer going to let my insecurities get in the way,
Because love is worth taking risks, and getting the most out
of each day.

Feeling Remorseful

When you drown in a sea of voices,
That replays in your mind.
You regret all of your choices,
While you're stuck on rewind.
Going over every word that was said,
Every move that was made.
Every message left on "read,"
Until the dialogue begins to fade.
Did I overshare,
Exposing all of me?
Why would I ever dare,
Because you don't like what you see.
Back to being private, I know,
Only shows what's expected.
A puppet is what you get for the show,
Only displaying what's accepted.

Toxic Love

Your love is like a toxin,
Running through my veins.
Clinching onto you is like poison,
That's unable to refrain.
You're my guilty little pleasure,
When I'm around you I cannot catch my breath.
I hang onto you like you're a treasure,
But ultimately, you're the cause of death.

Living In A Cell

You were my drug by choice,
The safest one around.
Every day I heard your voice,
With a soft and subtle sound.
You never left my side,
Even when I wanted you gone.
You constantly made me hide,
From dusk to dawn.
I only came to you for a fix,
To fill the void within.
But you had your own tricks,
When you lead me deeper into sin.
You knew what you were capable of,
That moment you showed me your face.
To a lost girl searching for love,
You swooped in to interlace.
Now you have me where you want me,
Stuck within your cell.
Just a prisoner trying to break free,
Trying to escape this Hell.

Sealed Lips

My lips are sealed,
Not a word comes out.
My heart is filled,
With worry and doubt.
I carry a load,
Too heavy to bear.
Down a lonely road,
Without a prayer.

Movement takes place,
But my mouth is muted.
My lips started to race,
But my brain is feuded.
Nothing coming out,
Not a word or sound.
A confession wanting to sprout,
But fear has me bound.

Get Off The Merry-Go-Round

They say you go in circles, always going around and around.
Never getting anywhere, just always being bound.
You take off with momentum, having goals on where to go.
But stumbling blocks got in the way, now you're back to what you know.
You've been there before, allowing disappointments to dictate your path,
Hindering your growth, you've already accepted your wrath.
They say you go in circles, never veering off course.
But it's time to change your destiny, by taking the wheel by force.

Defeat

You are my kryptonite,
You make me weak in the knees.
Sometimes I don't even put up a fight,
I just panic and freeze.
I expect my defeat,

Because I've never taken on another role.
Powerless and incomplete,
You've sucked the life out of my soul.

Loneliness

Sometimes I get too emotionally invested in those who don't feel the same way,
They show interest at first but move on the next day.
They go back and forth leading you on for the ride,
Looking for attention but putting all feelings aside.
When you no longer serve a purpose to fulfil their need,
You're left with heartache while they're liberated and freed.
Never give more than what's given unto you,
It's not real love unless they put forth an effort too.

Deserted Island

They say no man is an island yet here I stand alone,
Just riding the waves into the unknown.
I search for companionship, yet nobody hears my call,
People say, "Put yourself out there more," but ignore all.
So, I go on about my day with nobody by my side,
Just an island for now—along for the ride.
Hoping one day to find my missing link,
A chain reaction, just let that sink.
Having actual friends that stick around,
I once was lost but now I'm found.
Focusing on what road lies ahead,
Not my present state or the scars I've bled.
But the joy of what's to come,
The blissful journey to and from.

Long Lost Love

Have you ever mourned over losing something that wasn't meant for you,
The loss of a love that wouldn't push through.
The loss of a friendship that gave you purpose each day,
The deep bond you thought would never go away.
Have you ever mourned over losing someone you felt deeply connected to,
You thought you found your person, the one who accepted you?
But there was a shift in your relationship of who they were meant to be,
From friends to lovers, back to "what are we?"
They say you can't go backwards from friends to being more,
Expecting things to be the same as before.
So where does this leave us—at the end of our road,
Longing for there to be more than just memories bestowed.

Rejection

I'll never understand why people just come and go,
Was it not love to you that I would show?
Why are there temporary friends that come for a season,
They find a door without a reason.
It feels like they throw you away when it suits them best,
Like you were not good enough to stick around amongst the rest.
Making you question and reevaluate your every move,
Examining your worth and what needs to improve.
It's exhausting to fret over every closed door,
People always leave but I deserve more.

I deserve consistency, not someone who strays away.
I deserve someone who will always stay.
Someone who doesn't judge my every imperfection,
Someone to spare me from every rejection.

Finding The Wrong People

I search so hard to find a connection,
It's something my heart desires.
Longing for love and affection,
The kind of romance that inspires.
But what if everything I'm looking for,
Leaves me disconnected from You?
Closes every opened door,
And keeps me from breaking through.
What if I'm the one standing in the way,
Delaying what You already have in store?
Postponing that glorious day,
In search of something more.

I Give Myself Away

I give a piece of my heart to everyone who comes my way,
Wondering when I'll find the right match.
Thinking maybe if I love enough someone will stay.
Maybe someone will find me a catch,
Piece by piece I give it away.
As if I have nothing left to lose,
I remain incomplete to this day.
Waiting for someone to ignite my fuse,
Ready for someone to pour into me,
Give what I give in return.

Nothing more, nothing less you see,
Just the love that I yearn for.

Too Deep For A Shallow World

People reject you for your strong emotions,
They try to avoid anything that makes them feel.
Just going through the motions,
Denying anything that's real.
They'll try to bully you into conforming,
To become robots like them.
Rather than transforming,
They'll judge and condemn.
They'll make you feel less than,
And maybe a litter inferior.
When all along that was the plan,
To build the platform to appear superior.

I Can No Longer Keep It All Inside

Bursting through the seams is a floodgate of tears,
Gushing out everything I've held in over the years.
Everything I've kept inside,
Every unpleasant thing I felt I should hide.
Down a lonely road without a prayer,
Wondering if I called out if anyone would hear.
But when I speak nothing comes out,
Not a word or sound wanting to sprout.
Just emotions flooding the soul,
With no release to make me whole.

Just stuck at a standstill,
Waiting for Your touch to heal.

Falling For Friends

Are you afraid to admit that you might feel it too,
The tension between me and you?
There's an unspoken attraction between you and I,
But we always find a distraction, some may ask why.
Are we afraid to give in to what we both want,
Will it ruin our friendship, perhaps I'm being too blunt.
I'd hold you in my arms to make you feel safe and secure,
You'd never question my love, it's the one thing I can assure.
But for now, you're just a friend, a fantasy, one I can only dream of,
Until my manifestation comes to pass, hold onto that one day my love.

Hope

The sun will come out after every storm,
There's beauty in ashes in every form.
There's always a lesson when enduring pain,
A light that gleams after enduring rain.
Love that's worth waiting for after experiencing loss,
Peace after turmoil is worth the cost.
So I sit here thanking God for another day,
For the journey, He's taking me through in every way.

People Can't Heal You

You can't expect someone to restore you,
To put the pieces back together again.
Erasing memories won't do,
True healing must start within.
Write it all out,
Everything was left unspoken.
Even through doubt,
Realizing you weren't always meant to be broken.
You can be complete,
You can find peace within.
Just don't accept defeat,
And allow tranquillity to begin.

Fallen Stars

This is for the fallen stars,
The ones who lost their light.
It was dimmed from the scars,
That taunted throughout the night.
Constant feelings of rejection,
Lowering each platform in the sky.
Allow a moment of reflection,
To remind you when your stature was high.
You stood out amongst the crowd,
Shining brighter than the rest.
Because the opinions of others weren't allowed,
All that mattered was you were blessed.
This is for the fallen stars,
Get back up and straighten your crown,
Healed wounds are only scars,
That didn't keep you down.

Grabbing Onto Real Hope

You once were my crutch when I didn't think I had the strength to say no,
I held onto you for too long when I should've let go.
You became my identity when I saw my own reflection,
I gave you too much power rather than making a correction.
You took too many years that I can't get back,
But I found hope to get my life back on track.
I took control over how I think and feel,
I don't allow myself to be persuaded by what's not real.
Rational thinking and reasoning is how I win,
The fighter comes out from deep within.
You no longer have a narrative over my life,
I choose a path that's not dictated by anger or strife.
I can't go back through a door that's already closed,
I can't go against what my heart already knows.
There's a freedom now that wasn't there before,
There's peace now and I've already experienced more.
I can't settle for what is familiar and easy to get,
I must have a fighter's mindset.
In the end, the reward will be worth it,
Keeping my eyes on the prize and refusing to quit.

Alexandria Jett

Fear and Anxiety

Anxious Without You

I can barely breathe as my chest is getting tight,
I try to gasp for air but can't get past fight or flight.
I freeze up and get all tense,
Not knowing when it'll let up or make sense.
Because right now I can't rationalize how I feel,
Nothing makes sense or feels real.
Time keeps passing me by,
But I can't move forward and wonder why.
There's a heaviness that won't lift—wondering what I can do,
Life is weighing me down no longer having you.
I need to recharge so I can go on about my day,
So everything can be better and not in disarray.

Boogeyman

Sip by sip you drink away,
But it's only to take the edge off you say.
Fear grips me throughout the night,
I lay here pondering, will it be fight or flight?
I lay here with one eye open; afraid to make a sound,
If you hear I'm awake—will you come back around?
What will you do when you're not in a clear state of mind,
What are you capable of, I'm in a bind.
Flashbacks taunt me again and again,
Of my past life way back when.
I thought I outran the man in the dark,
The man who left scars, revealing every mark.

But there's more than one version of the boogeyman,
There are several monsters throughout a lifespan.

Foot In Mouth

Too many words spew out of my mouth,
Not knowing when to slam on the brakes.
Nervous shatter quickly goes south,
As the ground begins to quake.
I cannot take these words back,
So, I panic and ramble more.
Trying to slip through every crack,
To find an escape, a door.
Anxiety overcomes me,
As I dig myself into a hole.
Ignore what you hear and see,
Look deeper into my soul.
I mean no harm,
When my speech begins to fumble.
My words disarm,
As my feet begin to stumble.

Open Book

People cannot handle what is raw,
When it comes to emotions, I show them all.
I do not hold back how I feel,
I share my thoughts, all that is real.
I say what people are afraid to say,
Vulnerability each and every day.
No sugar coating or tickling ears,
I don't hold back, I overcome my fears.

I say what's on my mind and how I feel,
It scares some people when you're so real.
Some get uncomfortable and just avoid,
Dodge anything deep, try to fill the void.
But I lay it all out on the table and hold nothing back,
I need clarity to keep my life on track.

Don't Let Your Mind Deceive You

These feelings aren't tangible, it's something buried inside.
It's something so easily we often think we can hide.
It's feelings of doubt or fear creeping into your mind,
It's not forgiving those who were once unkind.
It might be a grudge we're holding onto,
Holding these feelings captive, like they're new.
But those memories that hurt you are in the past,
They are just memories of pain that weren't meant to last.
These feelings aren't tangible, you can't grab onto what you feel inside,
They're just raw emotions that you can no longer hide.
They'll eventually come out, bringing everything to light.
Because the raging war inside will eventually ignite.

Life Doesn't Stop

Life slips away from you because you took too long to heal,
You avoided every uncomfortable emotion that allowed you to feel.
That nagging pain and anger resonated deep down inside,
Revealed the scars and wounds you can no longer hide.
You lived in survival mode for far too long,
You spent your entire life trying to right those wrongs.

But holding onto it didn't free you from your pain,
Holding onto it held you captive to every chain.

Sleep Deprivation

Sleep is just a thing of my past,
When I close my eyes—it doesn't last.
Just a tease of how good you feel,
But when it comes to rest it's never real.
Longing to be close to you,
For once in my life, sleep the whole night through.
Side by side, throughout the night.
Like companions, it feels so right.

Bonus Mom

When life gets too heavy and I feel like no one's there,
I know I can count on you and a prayer.
Encouraging me to stay strong in my faith and trust in the One who knows all,
Because He's always by my side and will never let me fall.
You're the voice of reasoning to silence the chaos in my mind,
A woman of compassion—you're one of a kind.
Although we may not be blood,
It's never stopped your love from gushing in like a flood.
God knew what I needed when He created you,
A bonus mom so tried and true.

Loss of Love

Love That Didn't Push Through

My heart longs for what could have been,
Endless love—over and over again.
A life spent with you by my side,
Immeasurable adoration for the ride.
A bond so strong that could not break,
A connection so powerful that could not shake.
Intertwining souls becoming one,
Shining brighter than the sun.

The Storm Is Coming

My walls are slowly going back up, trying to find a safe space.
I sense a storm coming that's about to shake the foundation of "our place."
I look for something to hold onto, hoping for your hand.
But this quake is too powerful to see where you stand.
Will you look up and reach out to me,
Will the storm make it too hard to see?
I'm holding onto hope, that we'll make it through.
I'll weather the storm if it leads me back to you.

Long Gone

If you could die from heartache I'd already be long gone,
But disappointment happens every day, so I must move on.
I can't stay here in grief, moping around forever.

Even if our love story ended, it's something that was severed.
I hold onto hope—believing one day you'll return,
To have that love we once had, it's something that I yearn for.
Did you tell me lies to find a way out,
My mind has been racing and I'm full of doubt.
Did I put too much pressure on you that you just couldn't take,
Did I push and pry till you would bend and break?
Just be honest and let me know,
If it's time for me to move on and let you go?

Naïve

I was young and foolish, trusting every word you said,
Living by what was in my heart rather than what was in my head.
The signs were right in front of me, that this wasn't meant to last.
But I held onto every moment, hoping it wouldn't pass.
Love was in the air, allowing me to be as carefree as I could be,
Without hesitation, I opened myself up for you to see all of me.
Not caring about the risk, there was too much to gain.
I gave you my all, only to endure this pain.
I was young and foolish, hoping for the best,
I took a leap of faith anticipating you'd do the rest.
To be my knight in shining armor, to be my happy ending.
We could take on the world together, but I was left for fending.
I'd do it all again, to feel something like before,
But my mind is now opened, and my heart closed its door.

Alexandria Jett

Missing You

This pain comes in waves, fearing that I'll never see you again.
What if I never get another hug from you, it's too hard to let that sink in.
It gives me too much grief, I can't dare to believe that might be true.
I can't fathom the thought of losing you.
My heart breaks slowly thinking that may be my new reality,
I still hold onto an "us" even if it's just a fallacy.
They say time heals all wounds, but how can I just move on?
How can I imagine a life where you're gone?
Put one foot in front of the other and occupy my mind,
Focus on what lies ahead and not what's behind.
They say time heals all wounds, but for now, it's too soon to tell.
I'll try to move forward but can't yet say "farewell."

Dear Romeo

Right now you're my forbidden love and circumstances are keeping us apart,
But Like Romeo and Juliet, you can't mess with matters of the heart.
Just hearing your voice gives me hope of being with you in the near future,
It motivates me to wait patiently because our love will endure.
Our love is strong enough to withstand this test,
Our love is fiercer than all the rest.

So, I'll continue to wait because we can't deny our gravitational pull,
We'll find our way back to each other because life without an "us" would be so cruel.

Stronger Than The Circumstances

No matter what the outcome, I refuse to fall apart,
Even if the circumstances break my heart.
I know this pain will not last, so I have to continue to move forward,
I have to keep setting goals for myself to move toward.
I will allow myself a moment to feel what I need to feel,
It would be naïve to pretend what we had wasn't real.
What we had gave me hope that I could feel again,
It made me take control of my life, to finally begin.
I took charge and started to take a chance,
I started to believe that even I deserved love and romance.
So, if this doesn't work out, know that I'll be okay.
It may take some time, but I'll get there one day.

Alexandria Jett

Love

Self-Love

No matter the shape, complexion, or size,
You'll always be beautiful in my eyes.
Never forget that beauty starts from within,
And to love the skin you're in.
God didn't mess up when He created you,
You're His masterpiece, a beautiful view.
Take pride in who you are,
Because you shine brighter than any star.
You deserve nothing but the best,
Forget about comparison with all the rest.
You're one of a kind,
A rare gem, you're hard to find.

Sweet Friend

Is my love for you a little selfish because I like the way you make me feel,
Because I'm not used to someone being so genuine and real?
I have gotten used to your sweet nature, love in the purest form.
You're an angel sent from God, so sincere and warm.
You always have an encouraging word to give,
Without judgment or an ulterior motive.
You follow after God's footsteps to lead the lost,
By leading in love no matter the cost.
It's time for someone to pour into you like you've poured into so many before,

How can we be of service to show you love more?

(Dedicated to Lorita London, a true follower of Christ, who has a heart of gold!)

Grace

I didn't know what real love was until I held you in my arms for the first time,
I didn't know any other way to express the joy I felt inside,
so I started to write in rhyme.
Loving you brightens each day,
Shifts all the negative emotions and makes them go away.
You brought a purpose and new meaning of love,
The purest form was sent from above.
Watching you grow up has been an absolute pleasure,
An absolute joy beyond all measure.
I'll always be there for you through thick and thin,
An aunt's love doesn't run out, we're kin.

First Love

You brought laughter,
You brought love.
You told me there was a happy ever after,
That God sent from up above.
There was a warm embrace,
With a soft subtle kiss.
Every time I would see your face,
There was more and more of you that I'd start to miss.
To look into your eyes,
And glance into your heart.
A single touch brought butterflies,
With a single touch, you'd turn life into art.

I'd see beauty all around,
As wounds would start to heal.
You taught me to tear my walls down,
Because there was something much greater for me to feel.

Compromising

Love is about giving and taking and meeting somewhere in between,
I make room for you, you do the same for me, and we develop a routine.
Love is about compromising and its' best,
Finding what works for both, per request.
Thinking about the comfort and feelings of your significant other,
They'll return the favour because they don't want another.
Love is selfless in every way,
It doesn't put one's needs before another or go astray.
Love decides that teamwork is the only way to go,
Without working together neither partner can grow.

Our Fate

I wasn't supposed to be there that day,
I was supposed to be there the week before.
But sickness got in the way,
In retrospect, it opened a new door.
I wasn't complaining about the delay to start something new,
As fate had its' own tricks up its sleeve,
That day led me to you.
Something we know and believe.
The stars aligned when we both met,

The story boggles both of our minds.
It's something we'll never forget,
Because it's one of a kind.
We instantly clicked because we had similarities after similarities,
From punctuality to getting there before anyone else would.
To some, that may be peculiarities,
But to us, we understood.
I'll never forget the day I met you,
You were intrigued by everything about me.
How I beat you to work, is so true.
And how everything was natural and came to be.

Buried Treasure

I've waited my whole life to find a gem like you,
The buried treasure I had to get to.
There were some imposters that didn't fit the bill,
They were counterfeit, they weren't even real.
There's a depth with you, unlike anyone I've met before,
A strong connection that makes me want you more.
You are the missing link, that completes me in every possible way,
You are the destination of my journey—now and every day.

Real Love

You made me feel different than I've ever felt before,
Something I can't describe—you make me feel more.
My mind and thoughts are all over the place,
When you're nearby—my heart begins to race.
You give me butterflies like a childhood crush,

Feelings of adrenaline, you give me such a rush.
Deep conversations we have about personal growth,
We challenge ourselves as an oath.
To never be complacent with where we stand,
To chase after our dreams—we understand.
You bring out the best in me, you help me achieve my goals,
You completely fill in all the holes.
You fill in the void deep down inside,
Every time our paths collide.

The Strength Of Your Love

Your love overwhelms my heart because I never thought I'd find something so strong,
It's something people search for a lifetime to find, it's something I've waited for for so long.
Our bond is powerful and can't be easily torn apart,
There's resistance if anything tries to get in the way because you can't mess with matters of the heart.
We'll always find our way back to each other because what's meant to be will be,
We found our treasure together because our love has set us free.

Unbreakable

Our love is fiercely strong,
Something that won't easily break.
It's something we've waited for so long,
That nobody can stand in the way or take.
Our love is genuine and real,

Felt in every warm embrace.
It exceeds more than what we feel,
Stretched bigger than the bounds of space.

Take A Chance On Love

The reward is greater than the risk,
When it comes to you and me.
We deserve to see what real love can be.
Just how far we can go when we're side by side,
I'm ready for this journey, I'm ready for the ride!
The reward is greater than the challenges that we may face today,
Sadness will only endure for the night, but joy is here to stay.
So, are you ready to take the risk and see where we can go,
Are you ready for this journey to see how much we can grow?

You Have My Heart

I love you with everything I have in me,
Until you—I didn't know how that could be.
I've faced disappointment so many times before,
I didn't even allow myself to believe that there can be more.
Until I found my safe place in you,
My best friend—how our love grew.
You nurtured my heart so it could feel more than just pain,
You became my sunshine when I only experienced rain.
I finally experienced what love and happiness could be,
The moment our friendship blossomed, it was just "you and me."

I Miss All Of You

I miss your voice, our talks, and even your face,
I miss your touch, your kisses every time we'd embrace.
I miss you holding me and in that moment, I knew everything would be okay.
I miss all our talks about our "one day."
I miss planning out our future and getting out ahead,
But reminding ourselves to live in the present instead.
We'd still tuck away our plans for tomorrow,
While living in the moment because we knew time would be something to borrow.
We'd hold onto each other and say, "Always and forever,"
Because our love was too powerful to ever sever.

When You Came Back

Was it just a dream that I had you back in my arms,
Even if it was just for a moment, somebody sounded the alarms.
Everything that was dormant inside of me instantly became alert,
I felt your love again and forgot about all the hurt.
I saw a gleam of hope that everything will all work out,
I saw you in my future which laid to rest all of my worries and doubts.

Anniversary Of Knowing You

A lot has changed from a year ago to today,
You've helped me grow in every possible way.
You've encouraged me to go after what I never thought was possible before,

You made me realize that I can have more.
You cheered me on to overcome obstacles I once thought was bleak,
You showed me I had strength anytime I thought I was weak.
You made me want better for myself more than I did before,
Having you in my life has opened every new door.
You opened my heart to feel something new,
How beautiful life is, to be loved by you.

A Note From The Author

I have a copious amount of love poems, many more than this. I am not sharing them all in this book because I have an upcoming love story that I'm writing after this. Not to let the cat out of the bag, but the secret's out.

Alexandria

Spiritual

Why Am I Running From You?

Why am I running from You?
When You tell me to stand still,
Why do I turn?
Why do I think sin will be such a thrill,
When my soul's going to burn.
Each step I take is closer to the edge,
Everyone thinks my life is pledged to You,
But You and I know I'm straddling on the ledge.
One more move can end it all,
As I test the waters,
I ignore Your call.
What am I trying to find,
What am I trying to hide?
As sin has me blind,
Bondage has me tied.
Where am I to go with no hope in sight,
My soul's magnetized to sin,
Not an ounce of light shines within.

Unfulfilled

When you're running from your calling,
To fulfil a temporary pleasure.
You'll experience a great falling,
Beyond all measures.
A constant void deep within,
An endless hole you can't fill.
That's the price you pay for sin,

That's your destination when you follow your own will.
What will it take to leave all that behind you,
To lay your filthy rags down.
In exchange for something new,
In exchange for turning your life around.

Who Do You Say That I Am?

I come to you with unclean hands,
Made up of blemishes and flaws.
Barely hanging on by strands,
I'm down to my last straw.
I try to fill in the void by doing what feels good, but it's not right,
It leaves me feeling empty inside,
Invites darkness and dims the light.

When Will I Find Freedom?

I've been carrying the weight of my sins for far too long,
I've turned away from them trying to right each wrong.
Yet, all I feel is guilt and shame,
How can I redeem my name?
You covered my past with Your blood,
When will I feel your grace gushing in like a flood?
When will I be able to forgive myself for what I've done,
When will I not feel the need to hide or run?
Lord, free my mind from all of my shame,
Lord, be my redemption story and give me a new name.

Satan's A Liar

You call me by my sin,
When God calls me by my name.
You remind me of my past way back when,
And God frees me from my shame.
You hold me captive to my past,
But God reminds me I'm not a prisoner.
I'm free at last.
I don't live there anymore,
God opened a new door.
Your blood didn't pay the ultimate price,
It was His blood and sacrifice.
You tell lies and He only says what's true,
Why would I stay bound by listening to you?
He offers me the freedom that can make me whole,
You try to make prisoners out of every soul.

God's Grace

Your blood covers the multitude of sins,
Every wicked imagination deep within.
Your grace forgives every impure thought,
For the battle is already won that You already fought.
So why do I keep holding myself captive for every downfall,
Because when You went to the cross—You covered it all.
You knew I was going to mess up time and time again,
But through You, I can have victory over every sin.

Let Go, Let God

You're fighting too many demons on your own,
All battling within your mind.
He wants to tell you that you're not alone,
Just give it to Him whenever you're in a bind.
You were never meant to do it all, to come up with
solutions without a helping hand,
He wants to be there whenever you call,
To be a firm foundation on where you stand.
He wants to be the answer when you don't know what else
to do,
To not have any reservations about what He's capable of.
He wants to be the first one you run to,
To bestow peace and love.
Allow Him to calm the storm raging deep within,
Let Him be your serenity.
Don't divert your attention to sin,
Because with Him you can find your true identity.

Freeing Love

Love me through the pain,
Where the cares of this world disappear.
Where the bonds do sustain,
Beyond any anguish, turmoil, or fear.
Walk by my side,
Let my mind rest in You.
Where my heart does abide,
Because with You all things are made new.

Forgotten Treasure

I traded in my treasure,
Searching for something more.
But what I have could not measure,
To what I had before.
You were a promise that would last forever,
The only One known to be true.
The only One I would serve,
The only One worth holding onto.
I traded in my treasure,
Searching for something more.
But what I have now could never measure,
To what I had before.

Similar Struggles

We've taken the same path,
We've walked on eggshells trying to escape Your wrath.
With the same thorn in our side,
We understand that it's Your law we must abide by.
Follow every rule to a tee,
Complete freedom, You guarantee.
Life on the straight and narrow, we must stay.
Give us guidance each day we pray.
Put the pieces back together,
Through this storm, we must weather.
Keeping our eyes on You,
The prize is worth following through.
Extend Your hand and Your grace,
Give us the endurance to complete this race.

Relinquishing Control

Did I take the wheel and drive my own course,
Did I take back control without having remorse?
I prayed for Your guidance on which direction to go,
But I didn't hear Your voice to let me know.
So, I reasoned with what I thought would be best,
I took the journey to find happiness and made it my quest.
I still want You at the centre of it all,
Please take the wheel to prevent my greatest downfall.

Don't Get Distracted

You come at me with distractions of chaos and disarray,
To take my focus off the prize—you try to make me look away.
Your goal is to get me to quit before my calling begins,
Feelings of doubt and defeat before victory wins.
But I won't let the tests and trials make me fall apart,
To forget the purpose He gave me when He worked on my heart.
Sure—you're testing my patience by what you're throwing my way,
But after every test, I come out stronger each day.

Listen What Faith Has To Say

Anxiety tells me to worry about what has not yet come to pass,
Faith tells me to give it to God and fear will no longer last.
Doubt tells me to hold on to it because I'm not sure He'll make a way,

Peace tells me to relinquish control to Him and pray.
Our ways cannot compare to what He has in store,
We do not have the keys to unlock every door.
Only He has the power to decide what your fate will be,
So, take your hands off the wheel and He will set you free.

You're The Game Changer

My spirit craves Your healing touch,
The one that changes deep within.
My heart longs for things as such,
That releases the bonds of sin.
Only You can set me free,
Only You can restore.
Only You can transform me,
And make me whole like before.
But what's it going to take to get me out of my shell,
How will fear loosen its' grip on me?
At a standstill—I'm heading to Hell,
Because I'm paralyzed by anxiety.
There's a fear of failure that hangs over my head,
Because I haven't succeeded before.
Old wounds that I have bled,
Are still surfacing at their core.

Complete Surrender

I surrender everything and give it all to You,
Not my will but Yours, guide me on what to do.
Let me hear Your voice,
And help me make the right choice.
Because I can't stay here anymore,

I need You more now than I ever have before.
I need peace knowing that I am living right by You,
Help me follow Your footsteps in everything I do.

Make Over

When I step into the fire,
You take out all my impurities.
When I step into the fire,
I release all my infirmities.
The heat may bring discomfort,
Some say a little pain.
But how do you grow without a little rain?
Going into the fire, He moulds you and shapes you.
He makes you into His image and makes you brand new.
Do not fear the process, that's all part of His plan.
Step into the fire, and go to the potter's hand.

More Of You

I am thirsty for Your presence, the only thing that can bring change within,
A true spiritual cleanse, that washes away all sin.
You're the difference between what feels good now and what will last.
A peace that sustains, as Your blood covers my past.
I am thirsty for Your calling, Your hand of protection over my life.
Keeping me from falling back into anger and strife.
Encompass me with Your love and grace—to extend unto those in need,
Let me radiate a light, let me plant a seed.

Alexandria Jett

Stronger On The Other Side

Our pain is a part of our journey, it's not our destination.
It gives us strength and His restoration.
It's our testimony that we made it through,
Sometimes it's to shift our eyes back on You.
To allow Your will to be done and relinquish all control,
To allow You to mould us and shape us, till we become whole.
Sometimes heartache will bring us to our knees,
But it's not to harm us—let that put you at ease.
You never know who's watching you, following your lead.
If your strength, perseverance, and determination are the example they need.

A Note From The Author

I hope you enjoyed the many emotions of my poetry. I have had some heartache, but with God, I always came out on top. Sometimes in life, we bring more pain upon ourselves by trying to take the wheel and steer our own direction. Also, as you've seen through poetry, when I didn't give Him everything I was just lost and confused. I did not have peace; I was at war with myself. I constantly went back and forth in many areas of my life. When I finally made the decision to completely surrender everything to God, He brought peace to my life. I think many of us get hung up and always want to know why some things happen the way they do. Why did that happen to me? Why did I have to go through that? Why is life so hard sometimes? Just remember the scripture, "Trust in the Lord with all thine heart, and lean not unto thine own understanding" (Proverbs 3:5 KJV).

I also want to commend my mother. I love her dearly and I am so proud of her. In my introduction, I did not give you her story to disrespect her show hatred towards her or blame her for a hard life. Just the opposite, I wanted to give the audience an understanding of how Hurt people, hurt people and give compassion towards her because she had a difficult upbringing as well. My mom was always there for my sister and me, and she never left. She always took care of us and provided for us. My mom is strong and overcame numbing her pain with drinking. She has been sober now for almost four years. When I look at her, I see strength and love; no matter what!

Alexandria

www.ingramcontent.com/pod-product-compliance
Lightning Source LLC
LaVergne TN
LVHW021626080426
835510LV00019B/2772